You're On!
100 Ways to Shine
in the Media Spotlight

GAIL HULNICK

WINDWORD GROUP

Published by WindWord Group Publishing & Media
100 Bull Street, Suite 200
Savannah, Georgia 30401

ISBN-13:978-1-946527-91-1

Please contact the publisher regarding bulk orders, special events or speaking requests.
mailto:admin@windwordgroup.com

DEDICATION

For Stephen, Christina and Jacqueline

GAIL HULNICK

"The speed of communication is wondrous to behold. It is also true that speed can multiply the distribution of information that we know to be untrue."

Edward R. Murrow

CONTENTS

ACKNOWLEDGMENTS

To all of the people I interviewed, wrote about, reported on, and met
over the years...
To all of the researchers, story producers, associate producers, producers,
executive producers, camera operators, editors, radio technicians, and
station staff I worked with over the years...

I learned something new every day from each of you.
Thank you.

INTRODUCTION

When I started as a journalist, back in the day, the first on-camera interview I conducted was with a pro football quarterback who happened to be in town for a charity event, and who was kind enough to agree to my request to put a microphone under his nose. I was so grateful and so green that the story I filed included a four-minute clip of him talking about seven or eight different subjects. Not 'talking head', so much as 'blabbing on forever' head!

The assignment producer watched my first edit on my report, turned to me and asked, "Do you ever even watch TV?" It didn't go to air.

I realized that I had a lot to learn about the demands of the craft and the audience tolerance for boredom.

When I was in my first week of hosting a radio current affairs program, I was assigned an interview with a prominent classical musician – prominent to others, that is, but as it turned out, not quite prominent enough to me. I didn't do my research properly, assumed he was a conductor, and decided to start off the live-to-air interview by asking, "What is your favorite thing about being a conductor?" (In my defense against those who might suggest that is a pretty soft question, I have to say that it was a general interest show, not a music program.)

He answered, "I am a pianist, not a conductor."

Oops.

My comeback was "But would you like to be a conductor, someday?"

It was lame and I was embarrassed. I can't remember whether he was annoyed but I wouldn't have blamed him. I vowed never to be caught so unprepared again.

When I was covering business and politics I made even more mistakes. I learned from them, and from watching the skills of people who excel when the media spotlight swings in their direction.

Whatever side of the microphone you're on, the following tips apply:

Understand the medium and the audience.
Prepare.
If you're going to be in the game, know the rules. They won't change them just for you.

There are more suggestions I could make and many of them occupy the pages coming up next. Some will seem more relevant to the journalist, some to the interview guest facing a grilling in a crisis communication situation, and some to the would-be interview guest who hopes to raise the profile of his or her business or message.

I hope that among these 100 ways each of you will find a nugget or two that will help you in your work and in your efforts to shine in the media spotlight.

100 WAYS TO SHINE IN THE MEDIA SPOTLIGHT

1

ARRANGE FOR A "FIRST LISTENER"

N ovelists, screenwriters, and poets often cultivate a relationship with a "first reader". This person reads the manuscript in the draft stage and gives the writer his or her first inkling of how the material might be received.

If you're going to make an appearance in the media, try to find a "first listener" who will give you honest feedback that you can use to practice. Some people arrange for a coach, or depending on the relationship, ask their spouse, a friend, a relative, or a trusted colleague. One of your direct reports or your assistant is probably not the best choice!

Go to your first listener after you've written and rewritten your words, rehearsed alone, and made your answers as polished as you possibly can. Don't waste everybody's time if you're not ready. Listen carefully to every comment, and make the effort to incorporate and use the advice.

If possible, set up a reciprocal arrangement with someone who is also called upon to answer questions or do camera time in the media.

2

RECOGNIZE YOUR TWO AUDIENCES

When you are doing a media interview, you are not speaking just to the reporter. You are also speaking to all of the readers, listeners or viewers with whom you want to communicate. If a reporter seems hostile, uninformed, confused or even bored, keep in mind that the interview is an opportunity to go over her head to your "destination" audience.

3

THREE STRIKES IN A MEDIA INTERVIEW

You get your facts wrong. You misquote somebody. You lose your temper.
You're out.

4

NARRATIVE IS GOLDEN

Last week, an exec in a hurry asked for my best piece of advice in 25 words or less. Here it is, in four – "Don't give a speech."

He took it rather personally at first, thinking it was a judgment on his particular abilities. But when I added the next four, he saw my point: "Tell them a story."

Make sure there is a beginning, a middle, and an end — and that it doesn't take you half an hour to answer the question.

5

MARSHAL YOUR THOUGHTS

I f a reporter emails or calls, take five minutes or more to think over your responses to the questions you can anticipate. Try to turn a media inquiry into an opportunity, and set a goal for the conversation. As they say in the martial arts, if you aim at nothing, you are sure to hit it.

6

PLAN THE CORE MESSAGE

No matter what the subject, and whether it is to be a puff piece or hard-hitting journalism, there will be some phrase that clarifies the crux of whatever you are communicating. Identify it, then craft at least six other ways of stating it. Write it down on a note card, carry it with you, memorize it, and practice it. When a reporter calls or emails, or when it is time to write the story, you will be ready.

7

BE CONCISE

A sound bite in an edited broadcast news report can be as short as seven seconds. Try not to speak in complex, convoluted, or run-on sentences. Your comments might be cut off — or not included at all. Don't let yourself be carried away in your own thoughts and words, losing track of the time. Learn to use another part of your mind to run a clock on yourself and your statements or answers.

8

PLAN TO COMMUNICATE

If you are behind the eight-ball in an emergency situation and you have to answer questions from the media in half an hour, use the time to plan. Decide who is the best person to speak, what should be said, when you might see the best and worst-case scenarios and outcomes, where is the biggest and potentially most damaging fire to put out, and why you need to get onside with the media. Better yet, pull out the crisis communications plan you had the foresight to develop when things were calm.

9

SEE YOU IN SEPTEMBER

Newsrooms slow down in the summer months. This can make it difficult to get attention for your press release or publicity campaign, but in some cases, it makes it easier. The stories that catch the eye of the journalist working in the long, hot days of August tend to be seasonal, quirky, simple, or easily processed, so if your idea falls under any of those descriptions, go for it.

10

UNDERSTAND THE DIGITAL REVOLUTION

Just as the Internet and email revolution has had a profound impact on all of our lives, journalists have seen their world turned upside down in the past decade.

Take some time to assess these changes and how they might influence the way you approach and work with the media. For example, many reporters file for two or more different media and many different deadlines, for the same employer, in an environment in which communication is expected to be almost instantaneous.

This is why they seem to expect and to need instant replies to their questions. It's not a matter of arrogance; it's a matter of working conditions.

11

PAY ATTENTION — VISUAL

Take notice of as many details of the interview environment and the person speaking as possible. I play a game with myself, to ensure that I don't slip into daydreaming mode while waiting for an interview to officially begin. In your mind, ask and answer (any, but a minimum of) 10 questions — business suit or casual? Any jewelry? Watch or smart phone in view? Any other people around? Who and why? What's on the desk or the studio table top? Swivel or stationary chairs? Any logos or branding information to observe? Does the other person look focused or distracted? What's his or her first name, again?

Then, go one better and take it up to 11 – what color are his or her eyes?

12

PAY ATTENTION — AUDITORY

Learn to listen intently — and the first thing you have to do is stop talking. You would think this would be obvious but I've coached at least a dozen fresh journalists who think the best way to establish their credibility with their interview subject is to ramble on about their own ideas, opinions, and data. Not true. You do need to talk *with* people and share enough about yourself that you are there as a person, not a quiz machine. If you are the interview subject, yes, of course, you need to be articulate and forthcoming. But don't use that as an excuse to dominate. You will lose out on the valuable information that is there to be gleaned, if you know how to listen.

13

CRISIS COMMUNICATION REQUIRES FULL-TIME ATTENTION

When you have to tell Houston you've had a problem, you need to ensure that you have as much information as possible. You may not be able to wait until you have absolutely every fact, but make it your top priority to get ready to answer the questions.

14

STAGE FRIGHT IS A TOOL, NOT A FLAW

If you would rather face a line of massive football players (while you're down a couple of converted touchdowns at the half) than handle a hostile reporter, you are not alone. But learn to think of performance nerves as added strength for your throwing arm, and you'll be dodging the quarterback sack every time.

15

PREPARE

A detailed, strategic Media Distribution List is one of the most important tools to have ready for any media communications initiative. This List should be part of the Media Relations Plan, fitting in as part of the Marketing Plan, and including both a Comprehensive Segment, listing every possible outlet and journalist who might be interested in your story, and a Target Segment, with in-depth information about a select list of media outlets and people very important to you. Update the information every quarter.

16

FOCUS

When you are asked to do an interview, make it your top priority. Make sure you are clear about your message, your facts, and your point of view, and then set aside whatever time you need to practice for this situation. Once the cameras go on and the questions start to come, you should be firing on all six or eight or even 16 cylinders. That is the wrong time to begin thinking about warming up the engine.

17

DELIVER

During an interview it is easy to let your inner critic get out of control. We all have one — it's that private voice telling you that you're falling short of your goals (or goals that someone else has set for you). You don't want to let it take over — you need the edge that confidence brings. Claim a moment, as the interview is beginning, to consciously shut off that inner critic. Then listen intently to the questions and concentrate on your answers.

18

EVALUATE

Review your news media appearances regularly. Set aside time to identify and work on your strengths and weaknesses, preferably using the input of a coach or unbiased observer who can offer constructive suggestions for improvement. Ask others to review the quality of your answers and comments, particularly if you have any sensitive subjects to communicate or any legal issues.

19

DO YOUR HOMEWORK

Research everything you possibly can about the reporter and the media outlet seeking your input. Maybe in the 1970s or 80s people could dispense standard press releases to a faceless crowd of interchangeable journalists, but in today's environment you have to customize and personalize.

20

PRACTICE, PRACTICE, PRACTICE

Develop your own media training plan, and work it, just as an athlete does a physical training plan. Devote time to it every week. Then if you get a call from CNN, CBC, or USA Today, you are positioned to focus on that particular request, rather than realizing, with 20/20 hindsight, that you should have done something to get ready, many months ago.

21

IT'S ALRIGHT

If you don't have the answer to a question, it's completely acceptable to say so. Build relationships by offering to find out the answer and then emailing it to the questioner and anyone else who is interested. Follow through on your promise.

22

ONLY YOU

In a crisis communication situation, the role of the spokesperson should not be shared. Choose the individual thoughtfully, and weigh the advantages and disadvantages of having the senior leader take on this responsibility. The boss isn't always the best representative.

23

SAY WHAT YOU NEED TO SAY

Have you been in the situation where you felt blind-sided by a question you had not anticipated? Even worse, perhaps it was a question for which you really didn't have a response, because there just wasn't one that would satisfy the questioner?

Answer the question you wish you had been asked. Stay in the same topic area, but plunge right in with the information you want to convey. No apology, no retreat.

24

YOU GET WHAT YOU GIVE

Check out your own responses to the answers you provide. If you are bored with own material, or skeptical about your own comments, so your audience will be. Plan to be more enthusiastic and generous in your next interview, and watch for a difference in the response you get.

25

IT'S TOO LATE TO TURN BACK NOW

Watch out for the trap — the series of questions that back you into a corner. The skill you are trying to develop here is the ability to think three or four questions ahead, anticipating where the interviewer is going without looking as though you are picking your way through a carnival fun-house filled with obstacles and monsters waiting around every corner.

26

TIME IS ON MY SIDE

Good interviewers know how to use silence. If they hear any answer that indicates there might be more that could be said, *might* be said, or should be said, sometimes they just wait. One of the best lessons I was given, when I was beginning to work as a broadcast journalist, was "Don't be afraid of dead air." Anyone can use the same technique. Just stop talking, listen as intently as you are able, and wait to see what the interviewer or guest will say or do next.

27

RESCUE ME

If you ever find yourself the object of attention of one or more reporters or photographers on the street, the most important thing to do is walk, don't run. If you run, they will run after you, and if you are on public property, they are allowed to do that. If you stand still, they may surround you, while shouting questions at you. In either case, you look guilty and you feel very stressed. Keep moving, but *don't run.*

28

THE CIRCLE GAME

People are most likely to remember the first and last things they hear, so construct your answers accordingly. This is just another way to state a piece of advice given public speakers for decades: tell them what you're going to tell them, then tell them, then tell them again what you just finished telling them. A third way to put it — in your finishing moments, come back around to your starting point, and then re-state your core message, central idea or theme.

29

DO YOU BELIEVE IN MAGIC?

The best performers are capable of gathering advice from many sources. They process it, absorb the most useful inputs, and then put all the coaching to one side. When it comes time to step out on stage and show what they have to offer, they are able to be completely "in the moment." This is a skill you can, and should, cultivate for media interview situations.

30

AGAINST ALL ODDS

Confidence is one of the best attitudes to adopt, as you prepare to respond to media requests. If you step up to meet the microphones with a defeatist outlook, it's likely that your experience will be negative. Leave it to others to speculate about outcomes, if they must. For your part, just give it your best, and prepare for success.

31

JUST THE WAY YOU ARE

Gestures can enhance or sidetrack your statements, and if you receive advice that you ought to modify, amplify, or otherwise change one or all of them (and if the advice comes from a source you respect), then do change them. Unconditional approval is best left to the world of romance and "you're perfect, just as you are" doesn't help anyone become a master communicator.

But having said that...

32

MAKE YOUR OWN KIND OF MUSIC

Work on learning from the best, but only to a point. The way you think, feel, look, and sound is unique. Trying to copy someone else is sidelining your strongest asset. You.

33

SIGNED, SEALED, DELIVERED

Communication is a form of contract. When you go into an interview, you are pledging to the interviewer and to the audience that you are going to give your best effort. The best way to find out if you've held up your part of the deal is to watch for their reactions to your message.

34

SHOUT

No, don't — but don't whisper or mutter either. Work on your voice and on your vocal projection. Ask someone to give you feedback on how your voice comes across — in person, on tape, on video, on stage, and at the podium if you do presentations. Master your material first, so that your brain is not stuck in the track where you are engrossed in conveying your message. When you know your stuff inside and out, turn to improving your sound, if it needs it.

35

LET'S GIVE THEM SOMETHING TO TALK ABOUT

I f you are in the public eye, they will look for news about you. And although it has been said for many years that there is no such thing as bad publicity, this assessment only holds if you are obscure and unknown. If you do have some standards, and you want to avoid becoming the target of painful publicity, you will want to find a way to manage what is said about you.

36

HEARD IT THROUGH THE GRAPEVINE

Why not just use social media and ignore print, radio and television? The value in having a major news media outlet raise the profile of your name and your message arises in two very important ways. First, the credibility that comes from having independent parties sing your praises is very powerful, and second, the amplification they provide can save you a lot of effort. You need social media, yes, but you also need traditional media attention.

37

YOU CAN'T ALWAYS GET WHAT YOU WANT

Very few individuals or organizations achieve 100% positive coverage in the media. You will save yourself a lot of stress if you realize that no matter how hard you try (or how much pressure you put on the people in your organization whose responsibility it is to 'handle' the media) you probably will have to accept that you can't please all of the reporters all of the time.

38

SHOP AROUND

While it's not a good idea to play favorites with the media, it doesn't hurt to develop some understanding of which outlets and which individuals are more inclined to be aligned with your point of view or your interests.

39

ANYTHING IS POSSIBLE

D o as much as you can to prepare for the media glare but make up your mind that no matter what happens you won't be surprised. This attitude will help you develop a skill that is crucial for those who become famous or who have to manage crises as part of their work — grace under pressure.

40

WE HAVE ALL THE TIME IN THE WORLD

If you are responsible for communicating sensitive information to experienced reporters in a crisis situation, you will find that you are most likely to make mistakes or handle questions poorly if you allow yourself to be rushed. Whether in an interview situation or in your general management of the information flow, take your time and get it right.

41

USE YOUR FEAR

When the red light of a camera goes on, most performers, no matter how experienced or talented, feel anxious. Some say they get concerned if they are NOT nervous, because it means that they are missing the "edge" — that sense of readiness that is necessary if they are to go on stage or on camera, and really shine. So, if you feel a little apprehension about an interview, let it make you smile. It means that you have had that surge of adrenalin, and you are ready to go.

42

ALWAYS LOOK FORWARD

Don't get into a cycle of regret about previous public statements you've made or interviews you've done that have gone badly. That only leads to negativity, the blues, or even depression. You have far too much to do to get bogged down by the past.

43

SOMETIMES, IT'S COMPLICATED

In some situations, it may seem to you that it's just a matter of 'black and white' — that the steps to take are clear and obvious. You are spelling out what should be done, said or retracted, and everyone, including the public, should get that. But be prepared for others to catch on more slowly, and get ready to make an extra effort to communicate the clarity you perceive.

44

DON'T OBSESS OVER ONE NEGATIVE COMMENT OR REPORT

It is human nature to want 100% approval. Comedians will tell you that if they are performing to a room full of people and almost every person in the audience is laughing, they can't help but watch the one or two people who seem unmoved by the show. Perhaps it is an example of the "grass is always greener on the other side" effect. It's normal, but it's counter-productive to become fixated on perfection. If you put out a press release and most of the coverage can be evaluated as positive, don't dwell on the one exception. In the bigger picture, it doesn't matter.

45

THINK ABOUT <u>EVERY</u> PUBLIC WORD YOU SAY OR WRITE

These days, your statements last forever. If you give an interview to a reporter, your quotes turn up in his or her article, blog, or broadcast piece, then often are clipped, copied, pasted, tweeted, facebooked, linked, re-quoted, re-tweeted, and referenced in posts, articles, and search engine entries for decades to come. Whether news media or social media, the point is the same: your statements can be out there, for people to read or hear, forever. Imagine a yellow light seconds away from turning red — proceed with caution.

46

CHECK YOUR INFORMATION AND YOUR SOURCES

I f you are going to quote or assert facts about current news, a widely circulated story, historical events, or statistics, you could end up pink with embarrassment on national TV when an avid producer or researcher, armed with a tablet or smart phone, researches your obscure reference on the spot, feeds the correction to the host over her earpiece, who then uses it to make you squirm or put you off-balance. Talk about your own ideas, tell your own stories, and verify in advance any specific information you want to use.

47

MAKE SURE YOUR CORE MESSAGE IS COMPELLING

The competition for attention from the news media is intense. Yours is one of millions of messages trying to catch the eye of the public or the decision-maker. If the only shade you convey is beige, you'll never stand out.

48

BUILD UP YOUR MEDIA CAPITAL

Do you have a relationship with a reporter or blogger — someone you can call on for advice or coverage? One who will take your calls, answer your email within the hour, meet you whenever you have a question that requires face time? That is gold. Tend it, polish it, use it wisely.

49

DEVELOP YOUR INTERVIEW EQ

Clients sometimes ask me for a silver bullet against a bad interview or bad coverage. The answer lies in emotional intelligence. EQ is a skill that you can refine and polish with observation, of yourself and of others, and through practice. It is not a synonym for intelligence or IQ, and it doesn't arise directly from it. There are many different kinds of smart.

50

PEOPLE ARE INTERESTED IN PEOPLE

Even if you are representing a large corporation or a government department, even if your press conference concentrates on statistics, and even if you would really rather talk about things or events — realize that reporters are looking for the "human angle." You'll score brownie points that could evolve into major, positive coverage if you can cast your message and your story in terms that have a focus on people.

51

THOSE WHO FAIL TO PLAN, PLAN TO FAIL

If I had to single out the one thing to do, it would be *Plan*. In every interview, you need to have a strategy. Each request from a reporter is an opportunity — a chance to put your organization, your brand, your name, and your message in the spotlight. And for reporters, each acceptance from an interview guest is an opportunity — a chance to get your questions answered. It is much more than a simple conversation, and the risks and rewards are significant.

52

MAKE A MISTAKE TWICE AND IT BECOMES A DECISION

You have to take responsibility for your actions in your relationships with the media. If you "forget" to return a crucial phone call or email, or avoid a reporter once, you might evaluate that as an error and resolve not to make the same mistake twice. But if you ignore that call again, it's not "a couple of mistakes" — it's a decision. You've *decided* not to respond, not to communicate with that journalist — a decision that may have consequences. Perhaps that's a good decision, perhaps not. The important point is to be aware that it isn't just "a couple of mistakes."

53

OPPORTUNITY KNOCKS BUT ONCE

If you are asked for an interview by a major broadcast program, there is often a pre-interview. A producer, researcher or other member of the program's staff calls or emails you — not only to book the time and place, but also to run through some questions. Don't blow this off. It's not a waste of time and it's not an obstacle to the *real* interview. It's an extremely useful step, as you concentrate on the opportunity that's coming up. If it's a crisis communication situation, and you'd really rather duck the interview, it's still an opportunity. The pre-interview may take an hour or more, it may take 16 seconds. Long or short, you can be sure that your comments will be passed along to the host of the program, along with an evaluation of your strengths and weaknesses as a guest.

54

FLY INTO A RAGE AND YOU'LL MAKE A BAD LANDING

The first, and some would say most important, of the emotional intelligence skills is self-awareness. A media interview, like any communication, has emotional subtext and is much more than "just the facts." Your ability to decode and express your own emotions, while evaluating the tone and progress of the interview, will have an impact on the outcome. If you can't accurately assess yourself, and especially if you let anger get the better of you, you're probably going down.

55

EVERYTHING IS A LITTLE DIFFERENT AS SOON AS IT IS SPOKEN OUT LOUD

In my workshop "EQ and the Media Interview" I have coached people on how to field questions assertively. The process is to anticipate the questions, rehearse two or more answers, choose the best one, and then practice it. The key is to strive for assertiveness, without being aggressive, and to overcome the feeling of self-doubt that can lead to being bullied.

56

MARCH TO YOUR OWN DRUMMER

While teamwork and cooperation are important in any environment, you have to begin with strong players. If the whole is to be more than the sum of its parts, the parts can't be ineffective or needy. Cultivate independence in yourself and in the context of media interviews. Yes, it's important, even essential to consult with others, but maintain that stance of independence as well. In the end, the buck stops with you, and you are the only one responsible for what you say and how you say it.

57

THE WAY YOU DO SOMETHING IS THE WAY YOU DO EVERYTHING

List your skills and talents — what do you do really well? Drive a car? Cook a meal? Play tennis or golf? Most people bring intensity and pride to the hobbies or skills they really care about. Make a decision that you are going to bring the same enthusiasm to communication. You'll see results, and your self-regard will grow.

58

THE UNEXAMINED LIFE IS NOT WORTH LIVING

The debrief is the secret to continuous improvement. Painful as it may be, go back over your interviews and the resulting media coverage. Analyze them for ideas on how to improve. Self-actualization is the ability to realize your potential capacities, and is an ongoing, dynamic process of striving for improvement.

59

DON'T PUT OFF TO TOMORROW WHAT YOU CAN GET DONE TODAY

I f you are finding yourself on the media radar, whether for good news or bad, you're better off when you answer the call immediately. If it's a crisis, it won't get any easier, and may get worse, if you procrastinate. If it's a promotional opportunity, you risk having the reporter slip the hook if you take too long to reel in the line.

60

IF THE TRUTH WERE SELF-EVIDENT, ELOQUENCE WOULD BE UNNECESSARY

Take the time to prepare and focus, when you are facing any conversation that will take place in the public eye. Few experiences are more important and less likely to bring a guarantee of success — there are many ways it can go wrong. It would be nice if we could be sure that all listeners, viewers and readers will reach the truth easily and solely on the basis of your say-so, but reality usually requires that they receive assistance. Victory usually goes to the articulate.

61

A TIGER BY THE TAIL

While I certainly advocate preparing for media interviews and doing your best to influence the public attention you get, I also urge you to recognize that there is a limit to what you can do. The media is not a monolith, not a single entity that can be "handled" or "managed" or even "dealt with." It is multi-faceted and multi-dimensional, and is made up of countless individuals, making countless decisions. Therefore, you need to develop your ability to feel empathy. If you are inclined to prefer control over all aspects of your life, prepare to have that challenged. If you are in the spotlight on controversial issues, you may feel that you are coming out the loser in a fight with a wild animal. Sometimes, just recognizing that you aren't the strongest one in the room can help. Think judo rather than boxing.

62

THE HIDE OF A RHINO

Y ou may need one, if dealing with aggressive journalists or critical viewers, listeners or readers is part of your day. It might not be your first choice of a terrific way to spend your time, but emotionally intelligent people accept that socially responsible behavior and the ability to balance their personal preferences with the needs of the group are fundamental to the success of their projects.

63

GET OFF YOUR HIGH HORSE

Your interviews, your relationship with the media, and your public image will be much improved if you resist any inclination to view yourself as removed from or superior to your audience. Instead, see yourself as part of it. Your goal is to communicate and for that you need someone to hear and receive what you are sending. If you seem arrogant they may tune you out. Sometimes you may be misunderstood, and that's unfortunate, but don't set yourself up for communications failure by purposefully deciding to sneer at others. It's counterproductive and unprofessional.

64

BEWARE THE WILD GOOSE CHASE

I f you've identified a conflict with one reporter in particular or with the media in general, make a smart plan for solving the trouble. The easiest approach is to throw money at the problem but it's often the least effective, and if you've made the wrong choice for solving the difficulty you could suddenly find yourself a long way down a road from which it's virtually impossible to return.

65

LET SLEEPING DOGS LIE

Don't call after an interview to try to add or change statements. Occasionally, you may feel tempted to do so, because you are convinced that the interview went badly, the coverage is not what you wanted, or perhaps someone close to you has made a negative comment. What's needed here is a little reality-testing — the EQ ability to size up a situation accurately. Why do you think anything needs correcting? If you think the coverage is biased, is that true — or is it that you are biased yourself, and therefore anyone who doesn't agree with you must be against you?

If there clearly is a mistake by the journalist and a clear benefit to be gained by you in pointing it out, then by all means call and try to get a change. But if not, you risk the unpleasant discovery that you've drawn attention to something no one but you noticed anyway. In doing so, you may have damaged the relationship with the reporter.

66

THE LEOPARD DOESN'T CHANGE HIS SPOTS

Throughout the interview, pay attention to the cues and responses the interviewer gives you. The circumstances are unpredictable and dynamic — be flexible. Nurture the ability to read what's going on and adjust accordingly. Be personable, but be on your guard — the reporter is doing his job, not making friends with you, no matter how charming he or she may seem to be.

67

A CAT AND MOUSE GAME

If you are in one of these, hang on to your sense of humor. Do whatever works for you as a stress tolerance technique — deep breathing, positive visualization, exercise, meditation, extra sleep, talking it out with a trusted confidante, spending time with a hobby — anything that helps you keep calm. Alcohol doesn't work.

68

A BIRD IN THE HAND

While it can be a good idea to build an extensive, lengthy Media Distribution List and send press releases far and wide, it's often the case that all you need is the name and contact information for one media person — as long as that person is influential, well-connected, and interested in your story.

69

"NEST OF VIPERS," "BUNCHA MAGGOTS," "WEASELS"

If this is your opinion of reporters, you have adopted the "shoot the messenger" attitude, and it just makes you look bad. Reporters are immune to it, and sometimes see it as proof they are getting under your skin, or that you have something to hide. Control your impulse to call them names. It doesn't help, and it can damage.

70

DON'T PLAY OSTRICH

Even when you know that an attack of stage fright will accompany an interview, the worst thing to do is avoid the opportunity. There is just too much to be gained from doing media interviews. I know it can be hard to think of some interviews as opportunities, but it is a good attitude to nurture. It will help you resist the urge to run and hide.

71

UNDERSTAND THE AMPLIFICATION EFFECT

Reporters and media outlets pass along their information and spread the news. Practically every individual does these days. We had the Me Generation, the Boomer Generation, and now we have what I call the "Sharing" Generation (and what others have called the "Shaming" Generation). Be aware that a statement you make anywhere probably will be heard everywhere.

72

GET THEIR ATTENTION, THEN LISTEN AND WATCH THE REACTION

You may think the only important element of the interview is *your* message, and that it has to cut through the noise, loud and clear like a bell. Although it's correct that the message is vital, the decisive element in an interview is not what the speaker delivers — it is what the audience takes away. If they don't hear what you've said, then you haven't communicated anything.

73

MAKE UP YOUR MIND TO HEAR THE SOUND OF MUSIC

In the context of a media interview, the guests who arrive with a high level of the EQ skill of happiness bring the attitude that no question, no comment, and no technical glitch will knock them off balance. They choose their general mood, rather than allowing events or other people to dictate it.

74

"BETTER TO STAY SILENT AND BE THOUGHT A FOOL THAN OPEN YOUR MOUTH AND REMOVE ALL DOUBT"

This piece of advice from a bygone era is sometimes used to intimidate people into letting others (usually the one giving the advice!) be the only ones talking. Applied to the media, it limits the number of voices heard and protects a narrow power base — not a good result for the community. Applied to the individual, it fosters fundamental pessimism and negativity — the underlying assumption is that we assume that whatever is said will be foolish.

Bring an optimistic mindset to the interview (of course, it will go well!) and it probably will.

75

FIND FRIENDS WHO MURMUR, FRIENDS WHO SHOUT, AND FRIENDS WITH MEGAPHONES

There's no question that noteworthy attention and major promotion can be achieved through recommendations on LinkedIn, likes on Facebook, re-tweets on Twitter, followers and comments on your blog or your YouTube channel. And I do recommend that you have a comprehensive social media strategy. But don't underestimate the power of a major news media mention. The numbers may be much more significant than those you can rack up online. Plus, you often are speaking to different audiences — and perhaps people more interested in and suited to the message you are trying to convey.

76

PLAY YOUR ROLE

Don't look directly at the camera, look at the interviewer. If you look directly at the camera during a news interview you change the rules of the game —break the "fourth wall', in drama terms. You demand that the audience be aware you are making an announcement, that your next statement will be exceptional for some reason, and that you are cutting the interviewer out of the picture. You might use this technique if you are a police officer addressing a suspect directly or if you are a grieving parent trying to speak directly to a runaway child. It's like an alarm clock blasting you out of the best dream you ever had — it better be worth it, and it better be that important.

77

DON'T REPEAT ANY NEGATIVE QUESTIONS

In a media interview you may find yourself dealing with leading or confrontational questions. Don't echo the interviewer's question. If this is a particularly sensitive story, you may find that during editing the rest of your answer is removed, and it looks or sounds as though you are making a statement that confirms the negative news. Learn to bridge gracefully from the difficult question to the answer that you want to audience to remember.

78

BE AUTHENTIC

Most adults know (almost always) when something fake is put in front of them. If they don't know instantly, they have a sense of a false note, a melody that's wrong. In a news interview, whether you are the reporter or the guest, it is best to be yourself, be forthright, reveal as much as you can in the circumstances, and correct any erroneous conclusions or assumptions. Be genuine — but don't use this as an excuse for being tactless, rude, or cruel.

79

THE SOUND OF ONE HAND CLAPPING

You have to be honest with yourself about the response to your media appearances. You may believe that you did very well, but that is the opinion of only one person (and probably the most biased one!). Work on evaluation with someone who can be constructive and sophisticated in his or her observations and advice.

80

KEEP IT SHORT

There is a reason that a doorbell doesn't go on for five or six minutes. All you need to hear is the two or three seconds you get. Try to plan your answers to interviewer's questions correspondingly.

81

RESPOND TO YOUR OWN BIORHYTHMS

If your brightest time is early in the morning, don't accept an interview for 4 pm, if you can possibly avoid it. If you are nocturnal, don't agree to a live half hour at 7 am. Of course, there are exceptions, and it may be that the opportunity overrides all other considerations, or you may not have a choice. But if they do offer you one, choose a time that works for you.

82

BE AWARE THAT YOUR WORDS ARE VERY LIKELY TO SPREAD

I had a client who did a brief interview about insurance planning with a local newspaper in a Canadian city and had a phone call by evening from an aunt in Wisconsin who saw him quoted by name on the USA Today website. It was a bit startling for him, but no one could miss the positive implications for business!

83

DON'T TURN AN INTERVIEW INTO A SHOWDOWN

When the stakes are high and everyone is in crisis mode, it's very easy for the simple exchange of information through questions and answers to turn into a fight. Resist all impulses to see it as "high noon." Unless there is irrefutable proof to the contrary, the interviewer is not the gunslinger, he is the messenger.

84

ATTENTION IS NOT AN OFFER OF LIFELONG FRIENDSHIP

People who are interviewed or who provide information to journalists sometimes come to feel that they've made a new friend, particularly if the media person is sympathetic, kind, or even appreciative. Be careful here — it's no place for your midnight confessions. It's certainly alright to respond with sympathy, kindness, and appreciation, but never forget that the reporter's first allegiance is to the truth. The second is not to you — it is to his or her audience.

85

RESEARCH

Y ou can be sure that the reporters, producers, and editors are researching you, if they've requested an interview. It should be part of your preparation (or those of the staff whose job it is to support your news media efforts) to research the interviewer, the reporter, the writer, the program, the website, and the outlet. Don't act on your own assumptions — you could be wrong. For example, you might think it's obvious that no one is watching a particular program because it is broadcast in the wee hours before dawn but you might be surprised. Get the facts.

86

THE BEST QUESTION TO ASK YOUR INTERVIEWER

I f a reporter calls and wants to interview you for a story — and it *is* something you are interested in doing — ask him or her "what's your deadline?" Even in today's online world, where deadlines hit morning, noon and night, it's a question that shows the reporter that you understand his or her pressures.

87

THE SIGN OF A REPUTATION IN DECLINE

It is sad to see a successful person disintegrating from bad choices, with every misstep chronicled by the paparazzi. Most of us can't begin to imagine what that's like. No doubt it *would* be very tempting to blame the media, when your career is in its twilight — particularly if you think the media built you up and now is tearing you down. Nonetheless, you're more likely to be able to live to fight another day if you retreat at the right time.

When you're deciding when and how to do that, try to avoid focusing on details — "the media are on me for being 40 minutes late but it was really only 20 minutes" or "I was misquoted. They reported that I said I can't solve the problem but I said I can't solve the problem *quickly*." Those details don't matter and you sound like you're missing the point on purpose. Face up to the essence of the question.

88

THE MICROPHONE IS *ALWAYS* OPEN

Every year you hear new stories about people who have made inappropriate comments that were broadcast near and far. This is bad enough if it is intentional, but often it's just a case of someone thinking the microphones were off, and that the interview had not actually begun.

Always, always, always! 24/7!! Assume that the microphone is on. And so are you, whenever you are in any studio or in the company of any reporter, anywhere.

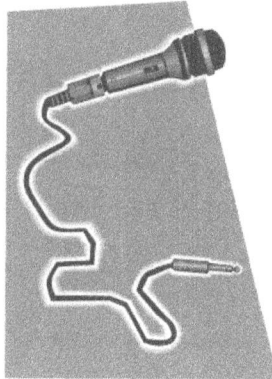

89

RECOGNIZE THE BEGINNING AND THE END OF AN INTERVIEW

The minute the conversation begins, start your engine and get going. You don't have unlimited time to warm up, and many people are surprised to find that the sun is setting on the interview just about the time they are getting comfortable. Be ready to roll, right from the first question, and once the interviewer is winding things down don't come rushing in with long, rambling answers that sound like a desperate attempt to hold onto the spotlight.

90

THE MEDIA STORM *WILL* MOVE ON

There was never a night that could defeat sunrise. No matter how intense the media attention and no matter how convinced you are that they will never leave you alone, eventually another controversy or scandal will draw their notice and your tempest will be over. Just hang on.

91

THE PAID INTERVIEW

C ash does not change hands in an ethical news media interview situation. If anyone is offering or asking for money, go elsewhere. Yes, I know there are lots of examples. And perhaps if it is not *actually* money, but it's just "help", connected to getting a really important story…

No. Let's turn the tide on this.

92

THE MEDIA PHONE CALL OUT OF THE BLUE

I'm often asked "what is the first thing to do?" I can think of 35 or 40 things to suggest, from informing your boss to phoning your grandmother to getting your best suit cleaned. But the absolutely first thing to do is focus on your core message. Plan it, rehearse it, memorize it.

93

THE MEDIA CIRCUS

If you wake up one day to find hundreds of reporters camped on your front lawn or in your office parking lot, with TV news vans and even helicopters tracking your every move, resist the completely normal impulse (whether you are guilty or innocent) to dash to the nearest airport. Try to see them as individuals, doing their jobs, rather than an uncontrollable mob. Find somebody to help you.

94

THE MEDIA TRAINING SESSION FOR THE NEW LEADER

I f you are the new leader, take notes and listen carefully to all of the advice. Even if you are senior and very experienced in doing interviews, you've never before been in *this* moment, facing *these* issues, or these particular reporters.

If you are the public relations, communications, or marketing staffer with the responsibility of providing the training, you have to call up every sweet note of tact, every gentle chord of diplomacy on your song sheet, while being clear and honest, and without letting the whole session dissolve into a mish-mash of office politics. Find ways to improve the leader's communication skill in this narrow, yet vital area, without giving him or her any opportunity to reject the entire task.

95

THE PRESS JUNKET FROM HELL

This publicity exercise can be excruciating for all parties. It can be torture for the interview guest to be asked the same questions, over and over and over and over and over and over and over again. It can be agony for the interviewer to be herded into a room, treated like a machine or a widget on an assembly line, given an unreasonable time limit, and yet be expected to deliver interesting and intelligent questions. Try to arrange a better scenario for both sides.

96

THE "OFF THE RECORD" INTERVIEW

If a reporter asks you to go "off the record," consider carefully whether this is to your advantage in any way. If you have news that you are determined to get out, and there is no other way to do so, then perhaps it would be a good idea to go this route. But make sure you are absolutely confident in your level of trust in this reporter. Find out the policies of his or her outlet with regard to naming sources and to informing supervisors about the details of the news gathering process on a particular story. Find out if there is anyone who can rescind his promise of confidentiality.

If you are the one asking to go off the record, you have to ask at the beginning of the interview or the specific statement you're about to make. You can't insist that it was off the record after it has already been said on the record.

97

RESIST THE URGE TO SAY "NO COMMENT"

Avoid this if you can — it's a phrase that's like waving a red flag at a bull, driving him to lunacy. If a reporter hears "no comment," he or she assumes there *is* something to be uncovered, and your urge to run and hide calls up their urge to chase. There are many ways to say nothing and duck a question without using "no comment." Practice them, if you think you might need them.

98

THE PRESS RELEASE THAT GETS NO RESPONSE

Investigate the reasons for this result, rather than just blaming the media for being too biased or too obtuse to come flocking to your door. It could be that it is poorly written, it could be that it's misdirected, or it could be that it just isn't a story.

99

THE NIGHTMARE SCENARIO — CLOTHING MALFUNCTION, PRODUCT FAIL, CAREER-ENDING FIASCO

Three words — maintain your cool. I've watched quite a few performers recover from a revealing moment, business executives explain a catastrophe, and politicians defend the indefensible. Many suggestions can be made about the best ways to handle it. Your first thought should be — this too shall pass.

100

THE INTERVIEW REQUEST AFTER YOU "GO VIRAL"

When your online fame takes a leap, you may find that your email or voicemail boxes fill up with traditional or mainstream media inquiries. Reporters get their information from many different sources and therefore it's a good idea to respond to these requests as quickly as possible. If they can't reach you they swiftly move on to other stories.

If your "followers" or "likes" numbers skyrocket, use this as a basis to send a press release to the mainstream outlets, programs or publications you'd like to have cover you. Be subtle in the writing and show the media reader why this is a good story. Next thing you know, you're on!

BONUS SECTION

Do you give a little more than you're asking for?

Stay in touch with reporters, even when you don't have publicity to seek, an unpopular decision to defend or a crisis to explain. If you only come around when you want something, you may find that it's more difficult to attract major media coverage, unless you are extremely influential or impossible to ignore.

I remember strenuously trying to arrange a brief sit-down interview, or a 90-second encounter in the lobby (even a chance to get some b-roll — anything!) with an important Saudi sheik who was in town for oil policy discussions. I was avoiding the assignment producer's calls and the unpleasant conclusion that I was going to have to admit failure, when a hotel staffer helped me out, sent me to the right place, and made sure I got my interview. I never forgot her empathy and her assistance, and would always make it a priority to return her calls.

How do you get started, building that sort of relationship with a journalist?

The Media Distribution List is one of the essential tools for generating interest in your organization or your story among reporters. Develop it, name by name and outlet by outlet. Identify the newspapers, magazines, broadcast shows and newscasts, online news websites, and any other outlet or platform that might be relevant to your communications goal. Find out the names and contact information for the people at those places who will be your channels to your audience — and don't be tempted to cut corners by sending things off to the generic Editor or Assignment Producer. You may find that their emails are standard (editor@, publisher@) but you should still address the person by name.

Checking the website of any media outlet is an effective way of identifying the people who can make the decision about your press release, interview, or coverage. Gather names from bylines, audio or video clips, read the lists of names from any About Us, Staff, or The Team pages, and look at the Contact page. (and there, you will often find very specific instructions for submitting story ideas or news releases, if the Home page hasn't already told you.)

Follow any instructions or help offered. It usually doesn't work to ignore all direction and blithely send your material off to the executive producer, the publisher, the owner of the station, or Richard Branson, because you have decided that you should be speaking to the key decision-maker. You aren't cutting to the chase and you aren't improving your chances of getting on the air or into the paper.

Unless, maybe, you are Richard's former dentist or yacht consultant.

Once you have built your Media List, keep it up to date. Reporters move around.

Be as personable and down-to-earth as you can, and try to treat journalists as individuals and as people, not just contacts on a list. Offer information, story ideas, positive feedback, and answers to any questions they pose. Recommend experts in their subject area or suggest good sources for their beat. As in any sort of networking, think of introductions you can make or help that you can give, just as often (or even more frequently) than you go looking for assistance.

The reporter will remember.

Camera Q: How to communicate using a lens and a microphone

When I was learning about television reporting and anchoring, our television prof was the remarkable Warner Troyer, one of the hosts of the seminal current affairs television program *This Hour has Seven Days*.

In one memorable afternoon, he demonstrated techniques for working with the camera that addressed each of our individual learning styles and subject-matter strengths. In my case, he helped me overcome a tendency to relate to the camera lens as some sort of opaque, black, concave wall, rather than a channel to a room containing one other person who wants to hear and see what I have to deliver.

He did it in about 30 seconds, using a sound check, a swivel chair, and a safety pin. And I've never forgotten the lesson.

I think of this as "Camera-Q" — an individual's ability to translate the thoughts in his or her head into a piece of communication received via video. It is a skill set, something that can be developed and improved, rather than a "natural-born talent".

Certainly anyone in a 'newsmaker role' might want to work on developing Camera Q. But we are now living in such a video-connected world that many other people are also finding that they face a camera frequently. Businesses are asking employees to participate in virtual tours, put online for marketing purposes; consultants and speakers are taping their presentations to provide samples on their websites; organizations, individuals, professionals, experts, and marketers all over the world have discovered YouTube.

There are many things you can do to raise your Camera Q, if you are preparing to do a presentation that involves a camera and a microphone.

Learn from the best. Watch television, watch online, and take note of the clips that make you feel something, that leave you thinking, or pry your attention away from whatever else it is you have on your mind that day. Watch analytically (and strike one small blow against television's tendency to sedate the spectator). Keep a list or a digital file of the interview clips, announcements, pronouncements, gestures, facial expressions, turns of phrase, and 'magic moments' that grab you and hold you. Use them for help when you practice and for inspiration when you are going to go on camera.

Talking on paper

At a recent conference, one of my workshop attendees approached me at the end of the session to discuss her biggest challenge – hiring communications staffers who know how to write. They had been through an extensive, expensive search process, found several people who could demonstrate skills in social media, graphic design, strategic planning, media relations, marketing and research. But when they took a look at the basic writing task they'd asked each candidate to tackle, they found no one who measured up to the standard required.

If you are looking for work in either business communications or journalism, you could climb a few rungs closer to the job offer if you improve your writing skills.

Writing is talking on paper (okay, on screen, too). And yes, you need to edit and proofread. If you have the resources, either in paid staff or in good friends who know what they're doing, you could make sure that every piece you send out has had a second review, a second pair of eyes to scan it, and a second brain to consider whether you've conveyed the meaning you've chosen.

But you also should try to move ever closer to perfection on your own.

There are many techniques to try, whether you are writing an attention-getting press release, a compelling news report, or even the next great novel.

But if I had only time to say one thing – THE most useful thing I've ever heard or read about writing – it would be "have a conversation with your reader".

Brain to brain, or thought followed by thought — it is always a communication loop.

For those of you literal thinkers out there – no, not necessarily a real conversation: a mental conversation, a virtual conversation, a metaphorical conversation. I'm not suggesting that a piece of writing is a group project or that the artist's independence and vision need be constrained or revised in response to anticipated response; I'm just saying that the "writer's voice" is always there, even in the most prosaic, simple press release. If it is just a whisper or a mutter, if it is ranting or incoherent, or if it is just plain bored with itself, the reader will have to work so hard to listen, he or she will give up and go away.

Try to think of your writer's voice as music. Practice it, polish it, and use it to make them hear.

We are experiencing technical difficulties

Recently I watched an excruciating live-to-air television interview with a Hollywood movie star. The program host, normally a personable, vivacious interviewer, showed her discomfort as his answers to her questions became increasingly terse, and then hostile. The actor, normally a charming, intelligent conversationalist, showed his annoyance as her questions (it must be said) became increasingly annoying.

The chat ended very quickly, with both of them showing their unhappiness and antagonism, and at least one member of the audience (me) feeling distinctly uncomfortable. As the show went on through the morning, the host mentioned the interview repeatedly, and eventually offered her assessment of the actor as egotistical, difficult, and unpleasant. We can only imagine what he was saying about her.

The whole thing started with a technical problem. He couldn't hear her very well — perhaps a headset problem, perhaps the environment in New York or LA or wherever the publicists had him sitting. His first answers were halting and hesitant, as a result. Then she jumped in, over the dead air. He became progressively more unsure and eventually she was reduced to saying "Tell me about your character" and he said "No, I'd rather people just go see the movie."

All in all, a disaster.

But no one is to blame.

Lessons to learn? Both individuals need to act and react with empathy at all times. If she were alert to the fact that he was in distress (or even just *might* be), either because of an inability to hear or see, or for any other reason, she might have handled the conversation very differently and have become less defensive. And he might have chosen to speak up and share

122

with her (and with us, his audience) his reactions in a more open, even humorous way ("I'm so sorry, I can't hear you" or "You're the 95th reporter I've spoke with today — could I just cut to the chase and tell you about the movie?").

Let me introduce you

I was recently asked by a workshop participant to identify the most important moment in an interview.

My answer was that brilliant, concise, absolutely definitive response: "That depends".

It depends on the nature of the interview, its purpose, its tone, its format, its style. It depends on the methods and identity of the interviewer. It depends on the goals and priorities of the interviewee.

The quicker answer is "the beginning".

People make their assessments in the opening seconds. Am I interested in this subject? Do I want to hear what this person has to say about it? Does he seem credible? Is it going to be worth my while to pay attention to this?

It is particularly significant if you are doing a broadcast interview. Your interviewer, the viewers and the listeners are sizing you up. Meanwhile, it's probably the most stressful moment of the interview for you, and can therefore be the most challenging time for controlling any nervous mannerisms or stage fright issues you may have.

A few tips: Smile. On radio, it will come through in your voice. On television, it will make you appear to be at ease and self-confident. If you are on camera, acknowledge the introduction with a nod and make eye contact with the interviewer.

Turn your body toward the host — don't leave it square to the camera and look over your shoulder, because you'll appear awkward, even dismissive of the interviewer. It may be difficult, and you may have to adjust the positioning of the chair. Get this all done before the interview actually begins.

If you are sitting in a swivel chair, beware! Don't let the chair move, even a fraction of an inch. It looks odd and it's distracting.

Focus on the host. Get his or her name straight in your mind, find out his or her eye color (not because there will be a quiz after, but because it's a good way to make sure that you are making eye contact), and get ready to pay attention to that first, absolutely crucial question.

The journalism mantra

I was in Washington DC recently to do some research and to tour Newseum, the impressive building on Pennsylvania Avenue devoted to the major news events throughout history and the journalists who have covered them.

On the wall in the entrance lobby is the quote from Rudyard Kipling that underscores the journalistic recipe for a thorough interview. It is a short poem about The 5 W's (and one H) and accompanies The Elephant's Child, from the Just So Stories (1902).

> *I keep six honest serving-men*
> *(They taught me all I knew);*
> *Their names are What and Why and When*
> *And How and Where and Who.*

Although the idea of these five or six essential questions pre-dates Rudyard Kipling, the concept is sound, and most journalists use the method swiftly and almost unconsciously.

Most would also agree that the most interesting question is "why?" It brings the most interesting answers and it often prompts a guest to think and to engage fully in the interview. As you try to generate a good question line, or try to anticipate the questions you'll be asked, make sure you include "why?"

It's also a good idea to try to think as you imagine an audience might — what would friends, your co-workers, or your family want to know? That's likely the way the question line the reporter uses will develop.

I've watched a few television news interviews lately where the reporter seems to get no farther than making a statement such as "the river is rising fast" or "you've been waiting here all day", followed by putting a microphone in front of someone's mouth. This is lazy interviewing. Maybe the reporter is trying to say as little as possible, and just stay out of the way, hoping the interview subject will be so emotionally moved by the event that he or she will deliver an amazing sound-bite, on cue. The problem is that it leaves the reporter open to the possibility (and I've seen it happen many times) that the response is "um, this isn't particularly fast" or "oh no, we just got here". Other times, it leaves the interview subject looking bewildered, as it's not clear what's being asked — if anything.

A few other basics: interview questions should be open-ended; interview questions should not be double-barreled; interview questions should not be answerable with "yes" or "no"; preambles to questions should be short, clear, and used only if absolutely necessary.

Listeners, readers and viewers want a secure sense that they have a grasp of the 5Ws and the H in the story. If it's about a complex subject, features some mystery, or highlights an intriguing person, they may cut you some slack before those questions are answered, but it's a loose leash, not a severing of all ties.

"A little knowledge that acts is worth infinitely more than much knowledge that is idle."

Kahlil Gibran

GAIL HULNICK

After 20 years on the air as a television reporter, radio morning talk show host, and newscaster, Gail began providing consulting and training services for reporters and newsmakers in business, the arts, and politics. She has an MA in Journalism, an MBA in Marketing, and an MFA in Creative Writing. Gail is also the co-author of two other business books and the author of four novels and a collection of travel essays.

www.ingramcontent.com/pod-product-compliance
Lightning Source LLC
Chambersburg PA
CBHW071428210326
41597CB00020B/3702